D0504265

Landlord Intelligence

The FK Guide to Being a Successful Landlord

by Finders Keepers Ltd

Copyright © 2015 Finders Keepers Ltd. All rights reserved.

First hardback edition printed 2015 in the United Kingdom

A catalogue record for this book is available from the British Library.

ISBN 978-0-9932585-0-3

No part of this book shall be reproduced or transmitted in any form or by any means, electronic or mechanical, including photocopying, recording, or by any information retrieval system without written permission of the publisher.

Published by Finders Keepers Ltd.

For more copies of this book, please email:
marketing@finderskeepers.co.uk
Tel: 01865 311011

Edited by Caroline Scotter-Mainprize

Designed and Set by RBDA Studio, Oxford

Printed and bound in Great Britain by Biddles Ltd
www.biddles.co.uk

Cover picture courtesy of Tim Hall

Although every precaution has been taken in the preparation of this book, the publisher and author assume no responsibility for errors or omissions. Neither is any liability assumed for damages resulting from the use of this information contained herein.

All of the information in this guide is published in good faith and for general information purposes only. Any action you take upon the information is strictly at your own risk and we would always advise seeking a professional's advice based on your individual circumstances. We are not liable for any losses or damages in connection with the use of this guide. While the information is considered to be true and correct at the date of publication, changes in circumstances and legislation after the time of publication may impact on the accuracy of the information.

FindersKeepers™

Welcome to the second version of our Guide to Being a Successful Landlord.

I say the second version as over 20 years ago, our Chairman Mary Channer wrote a ground-breaking guide which has helped many clients since.

We have written this new guide to help our clients. Many of our landlords are successful in their own fields and we see our purpose as helping them succeed in the art of being a residential landlord. We use the word 'successful' deliberately as people can form their own definition of it. For example, for some people it is purely income generation, for others it is their own home given back to them in good condition. Some people want to be heavily involved in the detail and some only want to see the rent hit their account each month. We are here to be flexible.

We liked the idea of writing this guide in a Q&A format. We asked every person in the company to each come up with the '10 questions most frequently asked by landlords'. Once we had removed overlapping items, this came to about 500 questions. We honed it down, coalesced similar thoughts and we were left with the 50 questions which comprise this guide.

I would like to say a big thank you to all our clients who have taught us so much and with whom we continue to learn about the industry each day. The rental sector is changing and our skills and expertise need to keep adapting accordingly.

The guide has the theory and our team are here to help you with the reality. I wish you the best of luck.

Dan Channer
MD, Finders Keepers

Contents

Contributors

Dan Channer: Managing Director, Dan joined Finders Keepers in 2008 as Commercial Director, driving the company forward. He quickly got to grips with the Oxfordshire letting market and excels at encouraging innovation within the company.

Mary Channer: The Founder of Finders Keepers with more than 40 years of experience in letting and property management. Believing that properties in the best condition attract the best tenants, Mary started Bricks & Mortar and Decorum Interiors to help clients improve their properties and increase rental income.

Emma Croft-Pearson: Emma joined Finders Keepers in 2003 and has worked as Property Administrator and Property Manager before taking on the role of Assistant Office Manager/Property Department Manager. She is now Office Manager of our Banbury branch.

Ben Procter: Ben joined the company as Summer Help in the Abingdon letting department and his potential was quickly spotted. He moved to our North Oxford office, progressing from Letting Manager to his position now as Office Manager.

Simon Tyrrell: Simon joined Finders Keepers in 1998 with experience in sales and property development. He spearheaded the creation of a separate Student Letting division and heads up the Property Management function of the company.

Frank Webster: Frank has worked in property for more than 30 years and heads up our Inspired Investment division, advising hundreds of clients a year on residential investment. You would struggle to find someone who knows the Oxfordshire letting market better than Frank!

Guest contributors:

Lesley Gordon, Jelf Insurance Brokers: With more than 35 years of experience, Lesley advises on and arranges landlord insurance, including Legal Expenses and optional Rent Guarantee cover. She also specialises in Household Insurance for owner occupiers.

Liz Higgins, Critchleys: With more than 30 years of experience, Liz advises individuals, families and partnerships on tax planning ideas and preserving their wealth. Her specialism lies in personal and business tax planning involving income tax, capital gains tax and inheritance tax.

Michael Morgan, TDS: Michael is the Tenancy Deposit Scheme's Director of Dispute Resolution. Having trained as a solicitor, Mike has been involved in dispute resolution for over 20 years. He joined TDS in 2006 and is now responsible for the management of its dispute resolution services.

Nick Walker, Focus Mortgages: Nick was a Founding Partner of FOCUS, responsible for all mortgage related business within the firm. Heading up the Mortgage Division which represents the largest specialist IFA mortgage broking team in the region, his specialty area is in Buy-to-Let and Let-to-Buy.

Assessing
an investment

1 What makes a good investment property?

First, do some 'homework'. Investing in property is usually about capital growth, so you want to choose a property where you expect prices to increase. You can also add value to the property by converting the loft, building an extension or even converting the front garden into off-street parking. However, before getting carried away with making changes, buying at the right price is absolutely critical. You should seek advice and research the market thoroughly.

You also need to ensure that the property will provide you with a steady rental income stream. This cash flow will make holding on to the property (your asset) more affordable, so you won't be tempted to dispose of it too soon to make a good profit. To make certain of a steady rental income, you need to know your target market, so that you can choose or alter the property to suit the demographics of renters in the area. For example, if it is near a university, then more bedrooms will be in greater demand than a large garden. On the other hand, a family home with a large garden and close to schools and parks will be more desirable if it is on a quiet street than on a busy road.

Do your sums – you need to understand the running costs of owning a rental property (insurance, repairs, tax). Choose the right finance, calculate and fully utilise any landlord tax savings – a good agent or tax adviser would be able to direct you – and also ensure you are able to cover any mortgage payments should the property be vacant at any point (during future renovations or unexpected voids).

A good investment property is attractive to tenants. As detailed in Question 18, the property should be furnished with your target market in mind, not your personal taste.

Lastly, find a good letting agent and property manager – and let them do their jobs! It can be difficult to treat a property as an investment (rather than your personal home), but a successful landlord is one who is willing to take sound advice and be flexible, ideally taking a long-term view.

2   How can I increase the value of my property?

Although there are no guarantees, there are numerous ways to improve your property, which should increase its value.

Some of the more expensive (but very effective) alterations include converting the loft into a usable room or adding a conservatory to provide extra ground floor accommodation.

Provided it is in keeping with the style of the property, an extension can add significant value. You can often extend without having to apply for planning permission provided your proposed extension meets certain conditions based on its size, position and proximity to your boundaries.

You might also consider converting a basement or adjoining garage to provide a self-contained 'granny' or 'nanny' flat. Although this can be expensive, it meets a growing demand from single or first-time renters (and indeed some downsizers) who look for a simple 'roof-over-their-head', pied-à-terre accommodation.

Less expensive alternatives include increasing the usable space of your property by revising its internal layout. This can be done at a much smaller cost than an extension. Putting in a new kitchen (now an important part of our living space) can add to the value of your property as long as you ensure the price bracket of your kitchen matches the price bracket of your house. Opening the room up to join the garden for safe and easy movement between the two spaces can also add value. Energy-efficient heating and hot water systems are vital, as are modern bathrooms with quality fittings.

Simple projects such as paving the front garden or updating the front door will all add to the property's 'kerb appeal' and will in turn create a 'wow' factor, resulting in potentially higher rent and increased capital value.

3 Will letting my property affect my mortgage?

In short: Yes. If you decide to let your home and you have a normal residential mortgage, you must let your lender know.

If you let the property without telling your lender, you are potentially in breach of contract. This is because the mortgage would have been set up under a regulated mortgage contract based on owner-occupation. If you have let the property and are no longer living in it, you are no longer keeping to the terms of the mortgage contract.

Letting for a couple of years
Often, the simplest way forward is just to contact your existing lender and ask for 'permission to let' or 'consent to let'.

If you only want to let your property for a short time, perhaps because you have been posted abroad for a couple of years, your lender may be able to amend the mortgage contract to allow you to let the

property under an assured shorthold tenancy agreement for a temporary period. There may be some change in the interest rate, but, upon your return, everything will go back to normal.

If your circumstances change, and you realise that you want to let your property on a long-term basis, your lender may insist that the mortgage is converted to a formal Buy To Let / Let To Buy arrangement.

Letting on a long-term basis
If you decide at the start to let your property on a long-term basis, and particularly if you are planning to raise additional finance (perhaps to help you buy a new main residence), it may be more appropriate to remortgage to a formal Buy To Let / Let To Buy arrangement from the outset. If you do this, you not only set the mortgage up to meet the rules for letting the property, but also you may find that any new mortgage arrangements better suit both your budget and future investment strategy.

In addition, if you're going to move your existing mortgage arrangements to a new main residence, you would need a new Buy To Let / Let To Buy mortgage in any case.

Insurance arrangements for the property linked to the mortgage may no longer be valid if the property is to be let. It is vital that any insurance policy for the buildings or contents is amended accordingly. We can introduce you to a trusted mortgage broker.

4 What rental yield will I get?

'Rental yield' is probably the most important measurement in residential investment property. It is an indication of the level of return on an investment and is calculated by expressing a year's rental income as a percentage of how much the property cost to buy. For example, if you buy a property for £165,000 and you achieve a rent of £825 per month, then your gross yield will be 6%.

The 'net' yield takes account of fees, repairs and running costs such as service charges, maintenance costs, building insurance etc. Technically, you should also factor in the first year's acquisition costs, such as agent fees, Stamp Duty and solicitors' fees, as well as furnishing costs.

On average, you can expect a gross yield of around 4–5% for lower-value properties in Oxfordshire. The higher the outlay the lower the return as rental value does not necessarily keep pace with house price inflation. Put more simply: if you pay £1 million for a property, you should not expect a 5% return on it.

Immediate gross yields tend to be higher outside Oxford, but the capital gains – arguably many clients' first reason for investing – have been stronger inside the Oxford ring road. Ultimately, the success of an investment is about the combination of rental yield and capital gain on the property. Oxfordshire's annual house price increases have generally been above the national average due to the buoyant economy and shortage of property – basic supply and demand.

If you buy what is appropriate for the area and your target market, then this should encourage a good return.

Note: rental yields change constantly. Take advice on any prospective investment.

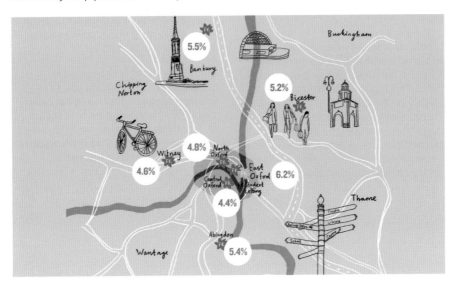

5 Which of your services should I choose?

Finders Keepers offers a range of different services to landlords. The service that will be most suitable for you depends on how much personal involvement you want in the day-to-day management of your property and your tenants. It is important to realise that tenants expect either the agent or owner to be contactable at all times.

Letting with rent collection
Letting with rent collection means that we manage the process up to the point when the tenant moves in. We also deal with the financial side of letting, such as handling the deposit and rent collection, but leave the landlord to manage their own Check In, maintenance and Check Out. This works well for experienced landlords with time on their hands.

Remember that if your property is not managed by an agent, the tenant will expect *you* to be available to respond to breakdowns or problems.

Letting only
Landlords frequently want to keep costs as low as possible. They are genuinely full of the best intentions as they envisage themselves looking after their tenants. So they opt for our 'Letting Only' service. This can work well short-term. Over the longer term, however, the responsibility can become increasingly onerous or – even worse – forgotten about, as the landlord is absorbed by other pressures.

We have often encountered the problem of a Letting Only landlord being abroad or out-of-contact when there was a serious breakdown at their property. The tenant (understandably) expects us to resolve the problem, but we don't have any authorisation to do so or funds to pay the bills. All we are able to do is field the tenants' anger and upset – extremely stressful for all concerned.

Management Service
If you are a landlord, and especially if you are new to letting, we recommend that you consider a management service. For the amount of work involved, this will give you much better value than the superficially cheaper Letting Only services.

In these times of cut-price offers, new landlords find cheap offers from other agents very tempting, but it is important to remember that 'you get what you pay for'.

As Senior Office Manager Colin Berry says: "It is often not until there is a problem that the true value of Finders Keepers' management is evident."

Our people are NFoPP qualified in sufficient number to ensure good emergency and holiday cover. We have over 99% rent collected on time across all our offices and virtually no TDS cases. Achieving this is not easy but the result of good training and long experience.

Letting and Property Management Services

WHAT'S INCLUDED

	Specialist Letting Only	Specialist Letting Plus	Full Management	Home Owner	FK Portfolio Club	Platinum
1 Initial visit to your property by an experienced Finders Keepers Manager	✓	✓	✓	✓	✓	✓
2 Assessment of your requirements and presentation of a marketing strategy to suit you	✓	✓	✓	✓	✓	✓
3 Discussion on rent level and advice on legal aspects of letting	✓	✓	✓	✓	✓	✓
4 Energetic marketing through your local office of Finders Keepers by specialist letting staff	✓	✓	✓	✓	✓	✓
5 Enhanced marketing through Finders Keepers' branch network	✓	✓	✓	✓	✓	✓
6 Prominent display on finderskeepers.co.uk of multiple photos, floor plan & EPC	✓	✓	✓	✓	✓	✓
7 Multi-listing with the very best property portals	✓	✓	✓	✓	✓	✓
8 Your property instantly notified to applicants by telephone, text message and email	✓	✓	✓	✓	✓	✓
9 Regular editorial and advertising by Finders Keepers in local and regional newspapers	✓	✓	✓	✓	✓	✓
10 Viewings accompanied by a member of our local letting team	✓	✓	✓	✓	✓	✓
11 Negotiation of all terms of the tenancy agreement	✓	✓	✓	✓	✓	✓
12 Comprehensive referencing procedure including a credit reference on your tenant	✓	✓	✓	✓	✓	✓
13 The bespoke Finders Keepers tenancy agreement, constantly updated with the latest legislation	✓	✓	✓	✓	✓	✓
14 Inventory and schedule of condition carried out by Finders Keepers' in-house specialists	✓	✓	✓	✓	✓	✓
15 Finders Keepers Block Insurance available at excellent rates	✓	✓	✓	✓	✓	✓
16 Holding of the tenant's deposit, registering it with the TDS, and administration of its release	✓	✓	✓	✓	✓	✓
17 Service of the correct legal notice as the tenancy end approaches, if required	✓	✓	✓	✓	✓	✓
18 Negotiation by Finders Keepers of applicable new rent level if the tenancy is renewed	✓	✓	✓	✓	✓	✓
19 Automatic re-marketing at least 2 months before the existing tenant leaves	✓	✓	✓	✓	✓	✓
20 Continuing expert advice from Finders Keepers as necessary	✓	✓	✓	✓	✓	✓
21 Property maintenance and emergency repairs carried out by the landlord	✓	✓	Optional			
22 Rent collection by direct debit with rent transferred into your account electronically		✓	✓	✓	✓	✓
23 24 hour online access for landlords to your property account		✓	✓	✓	✓	✓
24 Printed annual statement for you and /or your tax advisor		✓	✓	✓	✓	✓
25 Finders Keepers transfers utilities and council tax at all changes of occupant			✓	✓	✓	✓
26 Check-in of your tenant by your Property Manager from your local office			✓	✓	✓	✓
27 Check-out of your tenant by your Property Manager at end of tenancy			✓	✓	✓	✓
28 Inspections of your property, with photographs for reassurance or to spot developing issues			2-3	3-4	2-3	3-4
29 Negotiation of the deposit allocation, and handover to the TDS, should this become necessary			✓	✓	✓	✓
30 Finders Keepers maintain your property using our own skilled, proven contractors			✓	✓	✓	✓
31 Administering claims on Finders Keepers Block Insurance with our unique mandate up to £2500			✓	✓	✓	✓
32 24-hour Finders Keepers emergency helpline for the peace of mind of your tenant			✓	✓	✓	✓
33 Annual Property Appraisal meeting on-site with office manager, at your request			✓	✓	✓	✓
34 Seamless management of upgrades and refurbishment with Bricks & Mortar and Decorum Interiors			✓	✓	✓	✓
35 Project management of the sale of your property via our relationships with the best local estate agents			✓	✓	✓	✓
36 Vacant property management between lets, should this be necessary			✓	✓	✓	✓
37 Invitation to Finders Keepers' 'Club FK' events and seminars					✓	✓
38 Expert updates on the rental market and nationally relevant trends/new legislation etc.					✓	✓
39 Bespoke statistical reporting based on your portfolio's Key Performance Indicators					✓	✓
40 Annual sales valuation of your portfolio with advice about upgrades, investment and disposals					✓	✓
41 Notification of property investment opportunities exclusive to FK Portfolio Club and Platinum clients					✓	✓
42 Locum service – Whatever needs to be done, we will handle it for you, subject to our discretion. This can include organising airport collection, school visits, PA or valet service						✓
43 Discount on Finders Keepers Block Insurance						✓
44 Annual one-to-one meeting with a director of the business, at your request						✓
45 Rent guarantee insurance included						✓
46 High-definition film of your property						✓

6 Do I need an HMO licence?
What is an HMO?

An HMO is a tenanted House in Multiple Occupation. This means that there are more than three occupants who make up two or more 'households'.

A couple who are sharing with a friend constitute two 'households', while three non-related friends are considered to form three separate households. In both of these cases, if they were renting a house or flat, the landlord would need an HMO licence in Oxford city. A family of six people, however, form a single household because they are all related to each other.

Obtaining planning consent
If your tenants make up an HMO in Oxford city, then you need an HMO licence. But before you apply for one of those you need planning consent to let the property as an HMO.

Residential property is divided into different planning 'use classes'. Family homes have a class usage known as C3:

for an HMO this needs to be changed to C4. Oxford has severe restrictions on granting planning changes from C3 to C4, so do not make any assumptions. The process is, as with most planning applications: a fee, a form and a wait for the response.

Obtaining an HMO licence
Once you have the planning consent, you then need to obtain the HMO licence. This entails another form and another fee, and then an inspector will visit and tell you about any changes you need to make to fulfil the conditions of the licence. These are mainly related to the number of permitted occupants and fire safety. It is most important that everyone can get out of the building easily and safely in the event of a fire. So you will need fire doors on key rooms, a fire alarm system etc. We have plenty of experience of helping landlords meet these requirements and can guide you through the process.

Letting –
Finding a tenant

7 How do I know what the maximum rent for my property is?
When is the best time of year for the optimum rent?

The **good news** is that the answer is simple: the maximum rent is the highest price that someone is willing to pay at a given time.

The **bad news** is that rent values change constantly and some agents will bamboozle you with deliberately inflated rents.

The problem is that the estate and letting agent industry is built upon agents who:

1. Over-value properties to excite your greed and win the business. This means that you become 'anchored' to the high value.
2. Butter you up while the over-priced property languishes on the market.
3. Then tell you to drop the price to the level they knew it should be all along.

You also have some sellers / landlords who are convinced their property is worth more than it is and refuse to listen to their agent. Inflated prices mean that, if you are selling, your property loses credibility; if you are letting, you lose income – an empty property earns you £0. So what can you do?

1. **Research the market.** Use property portals to get a feel for 'asking rents'. But bear in mind that these are properties which have *not* yet let – the actual agreed rent will be lower as many are at point 2 above.

2. **Compare, compare, compare**. Ask your agent for evidence of similar properties they have let recently. If they do not have any, then you cannot trust their valuation – full stop. If they do, ask if these properties have the same parking / furnishing / quality as yours.

3. **Be honest about the quality of your property.** We all think our children are the most beautiful, but being too partial is dangerous.

4. **If you trust your agent, take their advice.** Look at the volume of competitive properties, how they compare, and the quality of *your* property and agree a first asking rent with the agent. Be confident but not naïve.

5. **Be flexible, be decisive.** If no viewings materialise after two weeks, the rent is too high. Reducing the rent will hurt, but successful landlords take action. They know they need to find the biting point of demand vs supply.

The best time of year will vary, but, generally, family and rural properties let best in spring and summer. The Oxford market is seasonal and rents are higher in summer due to the demand. Outside Oxford, demand for 1- and 2-bedroom homes is fairly constant all year round.

£3000
£2500   £3500
£2000   £4000
£1500   £4500
£1000   £5000
£500

8 How long should it take to let my property?

Why do you want to let your property quickly? Because an empty property earns you £0. However, there is no scientific answer to "*How long will it take?*" as letting successfully is as much an art as a science.

The best strategy is to put the odds in your favour by doing all you can to let your property quickly at a high rent while attracting a good tenant.

1. **Reduce the barriers.** Go round the property and tackle any issues which are going to deter tenants. The fewer barriers your property presents to viewers, the quicker it will let. This is a task which many landlords struggle with as they refuse to accept that some of their property's quirks may in fact be barriers! We have had countless (tactful and difficult) conversations with landlords explaining that the stained carpet / dirty curtains / 1950s bathroom is a problem.

2. **Make the property attractive**. Rather than just reducing barriers, make a positive effort to style the property. Tenants want value. They want the most quality for the price. If your property is appealing, it will rent faster and attract better tenants. So new kitchens, new bathrooms, redecoration, neutral and modern furniture – they all make a difference, if your budget allows. We do all this for many landlords through our Building and Furnishing Divisions.

3. **Be flexible about your tenants.** The narrower your brief is, the longer the property takes to let. If you say "no children, no pets", that is your prerogative – but immediately you reduce the pool of potential tenants.

4. **Get the asking rent right**. This is fundamental. As Question 7 shows, if your asking rent is too bullish, you will not get any viewings. Part of our expertise is to price properties effectively to hit the top of the demand. A classic mistake made by unsuccessful landlords is to become anchored to an initial, inflated asking rent and refuse to reduce it.

So if you do all this, how long should your property take to let?

You should have enquiries in the first week. You should have viewings within the first 10–14 days. If you have not had an offer within three weeks, action is needed.

When Bricks & Mortar (our Building Division) or Decorum Interiors (our Contract Furnishing Division) work on a property, our experience is that the tenant moves in immediately, once the work has finished.

9 Which websites should my property be on?

There is no 'right' response to this, but our answer is:

1. Your property should be on a large enough number of websites to deliver good quality tenant leads:
2. But not on every website, as too many leads can be counter-productive.

At Finders Keepers we pay property websites to list our properties in exchange for good quality tenant leads. At the time of writing we are focusing on Rightmove and Zoopla (and the many other websites they provide properties for).

We have experimented with many other property sites, but the quality of leads was poor. This means our staff wasted time with unsuitable people rather than getting on with the job of helping good people move into our clients' properties.

Making your property look attractive online

Having said that, just being 'on Rightmove' or on any other website is not enough. To attract the best applicants you need:

- Good photos.
- Good copy.
- The right rent – if you aim too high, good applicants won't even click for more details as there will be others offering better value.
- The right fittings and furniture (in some cases this includes the best presentation when letting the property unfurnished).

We find that a slightly better quality of applicant comes from our own website, **www.finders.co.uk**. This is because all the content on the site (e.g. Area Guides, Letting Guides) attracts people who then apply for properties*.

Photos of cluttered rooms will put applicants off even if you get the other factors right

Good photos with plenty of light and no clutter will attract applicants

Going offline to attract the best tenants

Often the best tenants do not come from the property portals. At Finders Keepers around 25% of tenants come from recommendations via existing tenants and landlords, referral partners and our relationships with relocation agents and big local employers.

For example, one of the biggest suppliers of corporate tenants in North Oxfordshire calls us whenever they have an incoming executive. Over the past five years we have earned their trust through delivering consistently, and we are now always the first port of call.

Conclusion

So it is understandable that landlords get fixated on which websites their property is on, and they are important. But if the property looks poor online, then your tenant quality will suffer. If you are not tapping into the local relocation agents and big employers, then you will be missing out.

* finders.co.uk was the first website to provide school catchment areas for each home (which won the Sunday Times 'Best Innovation' Award).

10 How can I get the very best tenant?

Successful landlords care about the quality of their tenants. Good quality tenants pay the rent on time, treat the property well, are reasonable with requests for repairs, and end the tenancy with the minimum of damage.

Finding the best tenant
The way to attract the very best tenant is, unsurprisingly, similar to how you achieve the best rent:

1. Presentation (see pages 38–42) – the biggest factor is the quality of your property. Good furnishing, smart and modern interiors, fresh paint and an investment in good repairs make the world of difference. Running through this landlord guide is a simple premise – *properties attract the tenants they deserve.*

2. Flexibility – the more you widen your parameters, the greater the chance of finding the best tenant. So be flexible with start dates, tenancy length, pets, furnishing and pre-tenancy works.

Can I vet the applicants?
We undertake the references and credit check which we pass on to those landlords who want to see them. If you want to meet your applicants, that is a

good idea, but be wary of scaring them off – tenants are sensitive about their right to privacy and the over-zealous or over-friendly landlord *("Hello, it's only me!")* is a stereotype to avoid.

Keeping the best tenant
You have found a good tenant – great. Now your behaviour will influence whether you keep them or not. This is why we are called Finders Keepers – because we 'keep' tenants and look after them. So we advise you to be reasonable and willing to invest in the property. If you hold back on repairs, your tenant will be unhappy – and there is so much choice in the rental market that they could easily go elsewhere.

I don't want X,Y, Z type of tenant, can you ensure that?
By law, you cannot discriminate on age, gender, race, religion, sexual orientation or disability[1]. Beyond that you can decide. We spend a huge amount of effort trying to match landlords' preferences ("academic couple") and that is part of the art of letting. As written elsewhere in this guide, the narrower your brief ("left-handed Scorpio with a cat"), the harder it is to achieve your target rent.

1   Equality Act 2010

11 Would I make more money doing student lets?

Letting to students has many benefits and some drawbacks. It is not just about money. You need to start by asking yourself what sort of landlord you are and what sort of tenant you want. If you have a strong emotional attachment to your property and want to see it loved and maintained just as you would, then it would not be suitable to let to students.

The money side
Students do pay market rates and, because they are exempt from council tax, they may pay more than similarly aged young professionals. Our student tenancies run for 50 weeks of the year. This means that you can plan for an annual income, which is attractive to most landlords.

We let student properties between December and March for tenancies that start the following August. This means that there are virtually no void periods and you can plan some way ahead.

On the other hand, students do tend to cause a bit more wear and tear than professionals. Standards still have to be maintained, though, so you may find yourself spending more on repairs and redecoration when you let to students.

Managing student tenants
Even the best student tenants will exercise their legal right to live just how they want to – and there's nothing you can do about it. Clauses in tenancy agreements can restrict some of the more unsavoury behaviour, but four, five, six or more students together are going to want to party.

The key to successful student letting is good, strong management. You're handing over your beautifully prepared, very expensive house to a group of 20-year-olds who don't really know each other and have never lived away from home before. We apply a light touch to let them play but a firm hand if things are getting out of control.

12 Should I allow pets?
How can I protect my home from being damaged?

A striking post-recession trend is the
growing number of tenants with pets
in the Private Rental Sector (PRS), and
the industry is struggling to adapt. Many
landlords do not understand quite how
many tenants now own pets.

Your obligations
As a landlord, you are under no legal
obligation to accept a tenant with a pet.
It is your choice. If you decide you do not
want pets, then the only consequence
is that you are accepting that your target
market is now narrower.

One important point is that we do not
advise putting pets into apartments and
most head leases will forbid pets anyway.
If you talk to animal charities, they are
not in favour of pets living in apartments
without gardens either.

Not all pets are equal
Some landlords are flexible about pets.
They might take a small dog but not a
large dog. They might try to find a tenant
without a pet, but accept a pet if the
otherwise ideal tenant comes along. If you
have soft wooden floors, then pets may
not be advisable.

Managing the risk

We often negotiate a higher deposit and work with the *Lets with Pets* guide from the Dogs Trust. It is full of common sense and, following their suggestions, we insert a number of clauses into tenancy agreements where there are pets, including:

1. We will retain £300 from the deposit two months after the tenancy ends in case there are fleas in the property.
2. We require a reference from a previous landlord or vet.
3. The tenant commits to a thorough professional carpet clean, including all upholstery, at the end of the tenancy.

Damage / Insurance

If a pet damages the property, then the tenant is liable for the costs just as if a human tenant had created the damage. Very few landlord insurance policies will provide extra cover for pet damage.

In conclusion

We understand that some landlords are worried about pets living in their homes. However, we believe the risks can be mitigated to a certain extent. We recommend being open-minded as the private rental sector is likely to see even more tenants who wish to keep pets in their rented homes.

LetswithPets®

13 Should I accept sharers?
Will I get more rent?

In many cities there is a demand for rented houses or flats from groups of friends who are planning to share. The sharers are usually young professionals aged between 25 and 40.

Am I allowed to accept sharers?
In the City of Oxford – and in some other local authority areas – you need a House in Multiple Occupation (HMO) additional licence if you are letting a property to three or more non-related people, e.g. three trainee nurses.

However, in some parts of Oxford no more HMO licences will be given out. So even if you want to accept sharers, you need to contact Oxford City Council to check if you are allowed to.

It is OK, I do not need an HMO licence
If your local authority does not require you to have an HMO licence, then whether or not you accept sharers is up to you. These should be the decision points:
*   *Your preferences* – Letting needs to work for you first. If your property has been your family home, you may prefer to see a family living in it. This is an emotional question, not a rational one.
*   *The rent* – Take advice from a letting expert. Sometimes sharers will deliver more rent as each bedroom will be contributing to the rent – that is why our student yields are high. At other times there is no difference between a family and sharers due to the shortage of family houses.
*   *The property* – Some properties just suit sharers and not families; for example, 3-bedroom apartments will rarely suit a family.
*   *Wear and tear* – Some landlords worry that three or four sharers in a property will cause more damage; images of 'The Young Ones' live long in the memory. In reality, most professional sharers treat properties well and you should expect wear and tear from *both* families and sharers. Basically, the more people there are living in a property, the more wear and tear you can expect. The Tenancy Deposit Scheme advises redecorating high-traffic areas (kitchens, bathrooms) every three years.

14 What is the ideal tenancy length? How long do tenants normally stay?

A tenancy agreement is a contract between the landlord and the tenant. Under current legislation, both sides need to agree to the terms of the agreement.

The main premise is that:

- For an agreed period of time, the landlord commits to giving the tenant private tenure of a property which complies with safety legislation.

- The tenant commits to paying the landlord rent each month and, upon leaving the tenancy, for any damage and dilapidation caused to the property.

So, in theory, you could issue a tenancy for any period of time. If it is beyond three years, then it must be executed as a deed.

In practice, 12-month tenancies are the norm, as they strike a good balance between guaranteeing the landlord sufficient rent and giving the tenant enough freedom to leave the tenancy after a reasonable period of time.

When we surveyed 600 tenants, the majority said they would expect a 12-month tenancy. However, we also issue six-month, two-year and three-year tenancies where landlord and tenant agree.

If the tenant wants to stay after 12 months, we recommend issuing a renewal tenancy with a new rent, e.g. with an increase based on the Retail Price Index.

But what if I only want a tenant who will stay for five years?

Despite what you read in the national media, very few tenants want to commit for five years. Most people cannot see their future that far ahead. As Question 8 discusses, the tighter your brief for a future tenant, the harder it will be to let the property.

How long do Finders Keepers' tenants stay for?

This changes with economic conditions, but a rule of thumb is 18–24 months. Since the 2008/9 recession, tenants have been staying longer due to the cost of moving and the difficulty of obtaining a mortgage.

The 18–24 months average is a blunt measure: many tenants move on after a year and we have live tenancies over 20 years old. We are proud when people stay for five years or more as it means our property management teams are doing a good job.

15 Why is my house not letting?
If there isn't much interest, what can I do?

If your house is sitting lonely and unloved on the market, there is a reason for it. Either the rent you are asking is too high and / or the condition of the property is not attractive to potential tenants.

As Questions 7 and 8 discuss, the **asking rent** is critical. A property is only worth (in sales and in rentals) what someone is willing to pay. So in most cases, if there is no interest, then the rent is too high and it needs to be lowered.

Of course, this is easy to say and harder to accept. It is particularly painful when the rent is near the mortgage repayment level and you risk having to top it up each month. However, the harsh reality is that some income is better than none – it is better to lower the rent, accept a 6- or 12-month tenancy and be left with 5% of the mortgage to pay rather than 100%.

The **condition** of the property is paramount. Tenants have high expectations. They want bright, light, clean and modern interiors; and that is why Decorum Interiors, our furnishing business, exists. Tenants will pay for the best properties and they walk away from tired homes. The properties in the poorest condition let the slowest.

You need to be realistic about the condition of your property. Often, landlords are too close to the property: they like it, so they feel that tenants must like it too.

However, you are not the tenant. You are not the target market. If properties are struggling, they need to be sorted out. At Finders Keepers that is our job. The changes we make can be minor (mowing the lawn, replacing vinyl in a bathroom) or substantial (damp-proofing a basement or re-styling the interior).

Two other factors may be at work: your soft criteria and the hard criteria.

The **soft criteria** are *your* preferences for how you let the property – whether you let furnished or unfurnished, whether you allow pets, children, etc. We have dealt with landlords who refuse to take their furniture out of their family house even though all of the potential applicants for that property have their own furniture.

The **hard criteria** are issues such as parking and availability dates. If the property is only available for six months, that makes it harder to let. If there is no parking available, it makes it even harder.

Conclusion: listen to the feedback from the viewings and take action. The more flexible and decisive you are, the more successful your letting will be.

16 How do you reference potential tenants?

The reason for referencing a potential tenant is to make sure that they are suitable to rent the property and will be able to afford the rent for the duration of the tenancy.

Most agents will use a professional referencing company who assess prospective tenants according to an agreed set of criteria. Most commonly, we take references for those who are employed and moving from somewhere else in the UK. These references confirm:

- That the applicant has a satisfactory credit rating – being registered on the electoral register has a significant effect on the applicant's credit score.
- That the applicant is employed, earns the salary as reported on their application forms, and that the salary is sufficient to be able to afford the rent.
- That previous tenancies, if any, have been conducted in a satisfactory manner.

Outside the box

There are many people who do not fit into a box in quite the same way as this and often we need to think more laterally. Those who do not fall into the 'easy-to-reference' category include the self-employed, retired people, students, company lets and those coming from overseas.

In these cases it is important to obtain as much information as possible. You can never be entirely certain that the tenancy will be conducted as you would hope, but the bigger the picture you can draw, the better.

Your rental property is likely to be one of your most important assets and if there is any doubt about the tenants, then it is sensible to be cautious.

Rent in advance and guarantors

If all referencing avenues have been explored and there is still insufficient evidence that the rent will be paid, then there are two further options. You can ask for all or some of the rent to be paid in advance, or have a guarantor to guarantee the tenancy. We take these courses of action frequently and they are a good investment of time and effort.

For those coming from overseas it is also important to check that they have the right to be in the country. The tenant should have a valid visa (if necessary) for the entire period of their tenancy.

17 Do I really need a deposit?
Why can't I keep the deposit during the tenancy?

A deposit is a sum of money paid by the tenant as a security against potential damage or unpaid rent.

Deposits are a major issue in the Private Rental Sector (PRS) and should be dealt with as seriously as you would treat tenancy agreements and gas safety records.

Do I really need a deposit?
We say a strong "yes". There are some landlords who do not ask for a deposit, but they are laying themselves open to risk and often are only waiving the deposit out of desperation. Paying a deposit is also a sign of commitment – it helps attract a better calibre of tenant.

How much deposit should I ask for?
This will vary. We ask for two months' rent for furnished properties and six weeks' for unfurnished. We have tried many different amounts over the years and we believe that our current deposit requirements strike the right balance between protecting the landlord's interests and being realistic for incoming tenants.

How do I register the deposit?
Since 6 April 2007 deposits must be registered in a government-approved scheme within 30 days of receiving the funds. The reason for this is to protect tenants from unethical landlords withholding their deposits without reason. This is good, common-sense legislation which has helped the PRS become more professional.

Do not be tempted to ignore this legislation. If you do not register the deposit with one of the three approved schemes (MyDeposits, TDS, DPS), then a court can order you to pay the tenant up to *three times* the deposit within 14 days.

Tenancy Deposit Scheme
member

18 What difference in rent is there for furnished vs unfurnished?

Furnishing is a major difference between sales and letting

Over 95% of properties for sale[1] are furnished by the seller, who is motivated to make the house look great. The buyer accepts that the property is to be sold unfurnished unless by specific negotiation and extra payment.

In the letting market, some tenants will expect a property to be furnished and other tenants will expect a property to be unfurnished. The decision to furnish or not is driven by the profile of the tenants and the type of property.

A grudge purchase

In letting, furnishing is a 'grudge' purchase. Landlords would prefer not to spend money on it as it is a sunk cost. The reverse is also true: landlords do not enjoy un-furnishing a furnished property (for example, when a tenant has their own furniture) as it requires manpower and incurs storage costs.

However, furnishing matters. Successful landlords put their energy into working *with* the prevailing tenant demand rather than fighting it.

To furnish or not?

This is driven by the property type and the market. We strongly advise that you listen to the market rather than become entrenched in your opinion.

---

1 With newly built properties it is different – normally a show-home represents the finished article and contracts are exchanged on an unfurnished property.

In our market, we know that Oxford apartments need to be furnished, as many tenants come from abroad without furniture. Outside Oxford we recommend that studios are furnished and larger apartments are unfurnished. Family houses are mostly unfurnished in all areas, though flexibility may be needed.

Listen to viewing feedback

These guidelines are not set in stone. If your property is not letting, listen to the viewing feedback: you may need to furnish or unfurnish to attract a good tenant. This can be annoying (see 'grudge purchase' above!), but with good negotiation we will make the letting work.

Family houses are mostly unfurnished in all areas...

...though flexibility may be needed to secure the right tenant.

Should I include appliances, crockery and bed linen?

- Appliances – yes. 99% of applicants expect good quality white goods as standard. If you expect the tenants to provide their own appliances, you create a barrier between your property and a good tenant.

- Crockery and linen – no. 20 years ago perhaps this was expected, but times have changed. We strongly recommend not providing crockery and linen unless you are offering short lets.

19 Can I furnish my property more cheaply myself?

Unless you have plenty of free time, like DIY and are very good at it, stay clear of the temptations of flat-pack or other cheap furniture.

Discount furniture is cheap for a reason. It is either out of fashion or end-of-line. Warehouse 'bargains' are usually more expensive, item by item, than single pieces in a complete coordinated 'look'.

Waiting for deliveries can be frustrating. You may wait in all day for something that eventually turns up at 5pm or, worse, you get a last-minute phone call to say that it will not arrive until the next day.

From (bitter) experience we know that flat-pack furniture is not as robust as fully constructed furniture. It can come apart unexpectedly and will not last as long.

Even the best quality flat-packs can be very difficult to assemble. One of our contractors counted 48 pieces involved in making up a double wardrobe...and it took 6 hours!

Ready-assembled furniture is a better choice, but avoid pine: it is inexpensive, but is out-of-date and no longer meets market expectations.

Moving up-market to John Lewis or similar is a better solution if you want to furnish your property yourself. Even then, what you choose may take up to six weeks to arrive – and that's six weeks with no rent coming in.

The bottom line is that tenants will never treat rental furniture as well as you treat your own furniture. This results in more wear and tear and more damage. The weaker (cheaper) the furniture, the less time it lasts.

Rather than spending £100 on a product that lasts for three to five years, would it not be better to spend £150 on a product that will last for 10 years?

20 If I accept an offer, is the tenancy guaranteed?

Most people agree that the property sales process is badly designed in England: either party can pull out at any time up to the exchange of contracts. Industry estimates suggest that up to a quarter of sales fall through before reaching the contract stage (this will be less in a hot sales market).

The process works better in letting. However, it is still open to exploitation by dubious / indecisive landlords and tenants.

An inadvertent verbal or written contract

A contract between landlord and tenant can be created verbally so any agreement before the tenancy agreement is signed and exchanged must be 'subject to contract'. In reality, a verbal contract is difficult to enforce, but it's a good idea not to make yourself vulnerable in the first place.

A written contract, such as an email, can be construed without a formal tenancy agreement and this can work against you, e.g. if you intimate in an informal email that someone can become your tenant and then you change your mind. So again, add 'subject to contract'.

When is an offer guaranteed?

An offer is only 'guaranteed' when the Tenancy Agreement is executed with both the landlord's and tenant's signatures. At this point both sides become liable for their obligations. If one party is delaying signing, then it should be regarded as suspicious and action should be taken.

A good process looks like this:

1. We (the agent) put an applicant's offer to you (the landlord).
2. We negotiate until both parties agree.
3. We confirm the offer in writing, stating that it is subject to contract.
4. We start due diligence on the tenant's references.
5. When the references are signed off, the tenant signs the agreement and then the landlord signs the agreement.
6. Keys are only released when all 'move-in monies' are received and cleared.

How many offers fall through?

Around 5% of our offers fall through once an application fee has been paid.

There are two main reasons for why offers fall through:

- *Poor credit history and references*
  A minority of applicants try to hide their poor credit history and it can sometimes be difficult to flush out credit issues before putting offers to the landlord.

- *Change of mind / indecision*
  People can be unreliable – they love the property one minute, then suddenly have second thoughts.

Good Presentation

Examples to illustrate what we mean by good furnishing and presentation

Mirrors can give the illusion of more space and can increase the amount of light in a dark area

Over-sized lighting can act as a focal point for a room. Use light to vary brightness and shadow

Use soft furnishings to refresh the scheme or introduce a new accent colour to your neutral scheme

Use rugs to define areas in an open-plan space

A well-designed scheme is timeless as it does not follow trends

De-clutter: too many things can look messy and distract from the style you're trying to achieve

Choose sturdy furniture over flat-pack; in the long term it is the wiser investment

Don't be afraid to layer patterns or texture, but make sure they complement each other

Use pictures and paintings in small numbers and always hang them at eye level

Create a neutral palette and let the soft furnishings provide the mix of patterns or colours, avoiding personal tastes for rental properties

Letting –
Getting your property ready

21 What do I need to do to prepare my property for letting?

The amount of work will vary depending on the condition of the property. Everything needs to be in good repair and working order. To take two examples at opposite extremes:

Preparing a new 2-bedroom flat

- Organise professional cleaning, including windows inside and outside; check smoke alarm batteries, window lock keys and that trickle vents on windows open properly.
- Make sure you know the new postcode.
- Supply – if unfurnished and not already fitted:

  ✓ Washing machine, tumble dryer or washer dryer, fridge, freezer, light fittings, curtains or blinds to fit windows, carpet; water-repellent flooring in the kitchen and bathroom.

- As a courtesy also include:

  ✓ Internal and external doormats to protect your floors, WC brushes, cleaning materials, dustbins, WC paper.

In a well lived-in family house, there can be a much larger to-do list that includes details such as:

- Sweeping flues / chimneys
- Measuring oil in the tank (leave a reasonable minimum)
- Replacing light fittings, supplying various different light bulbs
- Organising repairs needed: electrician for electrical safety test, decorator or plumber
- Pressure-hosing the patios

- Pruning shrubs
- Working over the garden / final grass-cutting
- Removing children's outdoor toys and bikes
- Replacing the odd carpet or curtain

At Finders Keepers we can handle all or some of this preparation work – as much as suits you.

If you opt to control everything yourself, we advise working to at least a 48-hour margin (and preferably 72 hours) before the tenancy starts. We find that landlords often run out of time as they are unable to concentrate solely on preparing their properties for letting.

The inventory can only be taken once the property is 100% ready. It must then be typed up before the tenancy begins and given to the tenant on the first day.

22 What do I do about gas safety? Is electrical safety a legal requirement?

Gas Safety Checks are the most important item of compliance and should be taken extremely seriously.

Gas Safety Regulations 1998 require a landlord to have a gas safety check carried out annually. Appliances, flues and pipework must be safety-checked and a record provided. We currently organise 1,400 gas safety checks a year via Bricks & Mortar, our building division.

Occasionally issues are found at the first check, and this is most common when a landlord lets their own home. This is because, whilst homeowners *should* use a Gas Safe engineer for any work relating to gas in the property, nobody polices this. You might have been living in your home for years with no problems – but it still might not be up to the standards required by law when you let the property. We've had a few difficult conversations with landlords about this over the years, but the law is clear. Any remedial work must be carried out.

Failure to do so is a criminal offence carrying a maximum prison term of six months and a fine of £5,000. More seriously though, if anything were to happen to a tenant during a tenancy, the penalties could be far more severe. A manslaughter charge is not an attractive proposition.

It's not a legal requirement to have a full electrical safety check carried out on non-HMO properties, but it is a legal requirement to show due diligence. At Finders Keepers we therefore insist that an electrical safety check is carried out on all properties.

This probably seems like just one more task to add to the apparently endless list of things to do when you start letting a property. But experience has taught us that doing everything correctly at the beginning results in fewer risks to you.

Various regulations insist that systems must be safely installed and maintained. Our view is that you can only be sure of this by having a qualified, industry-approved electrician check the installation. There was recently a fire at a property we manage. The first question the fire officer asked was: "Have you had an electrical safety check carried out?" Need we say more?

The cost of an electrical safety check is relatively small, depending on the size and age of the property, and the condition of the electrical installation. The certificate typically lasts for five years.

A PAT test is different and consists of a check of the electrical items in a property, most commonly kitchen appliances. These should ideally be checked annually by a competent person according to the Electrical Equipment (Safety) Regulations 1994.

23 What are my legal responsibilities as a landlord?

There is a misconception that it is easy to be a successful landlord. It is not; that is why specialists exist who deal with problems day-in, day-out and understand the legal obligations.

Landlord and Tenant Act 1985
To keep in working order:

- The structure and exterior of the property (including gutters, drains and pipes)
- Installations for the supply of water, electricity and gas
- Sanitary appliances: basins, sinks, baths
- Space heating and water heating

Gas Safety Regulations 1998
To carry out an annual gas safety check by a Gas Safe registered engineer.

Furniture and Furnishings (Fire Safety) Regulations 1993
To use in a rental property only furniture that is compliant with fire safety regulations and has passed the required match tests.

Electrical Equipment Regulations 1994
Electrical items in a property should be checked annually by an accredited electrician.

Part P Building Regulations
Many types of electrical work in dwellings must be approved by the local authority building control department or carried out by an electrician who is fully Part P compliant and a member of BSI, Elecsa, NICEIC or NAPIT.

Part 6 of the Housing Act 2004
The deposit on an assured shorthold tenancy must be protected by the landlord. It must be held by someone who belongs to a recognised insurance scheme or be paid into a custodial scheme.

Energy Performance of Buildings Regulations 2008
An Energy Performance Certificate must be carried out for all properties that are marketed to let.

Non Resident Landlord Taxes 2007
You must advise HMRC if you will be overseas for a period of time and letting a property.

Protection from Eviction Act 1977
The landlord may not harass the tenant, enter the property without their permission, or change the locks without their knowledge.

There are contractual responsibilities too such as allowing the tenant quiet enjoyment of the property, proving you have consent to let from your mortgage provider or leaseholder, and insuring the property.

24 Can I retain somewhere in the house or garage to store my stuff?

Yes: it is *your* house! The rental contract between landlord and tenant is a negotiation. You can include any reasonable and legal clauses provided both parties agree.

It is worth considering that if you retain part of the house for storing your possessions you may be liable to pay some or all of the council tax. Please check with your local authority.

On the whole we actually advise against trying to keep your possessions in the property for a number of reasons.

- Invariably it is in that locked garage / loft / room that a problem arises, whether it is vermin, burst pipes or just needing access to it for faulty wiring.

- If the agent holds the key and the problem occurs out of working hours, there can be a delay in locating the key from the office. On the other hand, if the key is hidden at the property (the best solution), the agent must remember its location and make sure that the tenant doesn't find out. If the tenant knows, then the agent loses control on the landlord's behalf.

- Control can be lost anyway. We have known (through discovery or Check Out tenant confession) tenants who 'broke in' for whatever reason anyway. So never assume total security.

- Even if none of these scenarios occurs, tenants often resent being excluded from a part of their rental home, especially the loft or garage.

25 Who maintains the garden?

Gardens cause problems. Landlords tend to care a lot about their gardens, yet most tenants are not good gardeners, particularly if they are often away on business or have a home elsewhere in the UK.

Indeed, over the past five years we have noticed that tenants have fewer and fewer gardening skills.

This is our view on managing gardens:

- If the garden maintenance is important to you or if it is a big garden, a gardener should be employed and paid by you and we will hope to add this cost to the rent. This forms part of the negotiation when agreeing the terms of the tenancy. We do this often and it works well.

- During the growing season we check that the lawn is cut regularly – as far as possible.

- Compromises can be reached. For example, a landlord commits to taking care of trees, shrubs and flowers and the tenant takes care of the leaves and the lawn.

- Tenants can't be held responsible if one or more plants die.

- We include photographs of the garden on the inventory and will do our best to ensure that we hand it back to you in similar condition, even if this involves charging the tenant, which requires his or her consent.

- Gardens grow. If you have not seen your property for a few years, then sometimes drastic action can be needed: for example, cutting back a tree that is dangerous or diseased.

26 Do I really need the property professionally cleaned before and after tenancies?

Yes. At Finders Keepers, our standard is 'hotel clean'. Otherwise, as we know from experience, the incoming tenant will complain and refuse to employ professional cleaners before vacating. We have a detailed Check In form for this purpose which includes the statement, "I agree that the property is thoroughly clean."

Carpets need to be *professionally* cleaned. Amateur DIY machines are not good enough.

If the tenancy starts well, with the tenant satisfied, it is likely to proceed well. If it starts badly, even if there is some form of financial compensation, it becomes tainted by resentment. A tenancy spoiled by any sort of negative emotion is not a successful one.

Since we introduced pre-Check Out appointments to remind tenants of their obligations and suggest professional cleaning companies, disputes at the Check Out stage have greatly reduced.

So starting well should ensure that the outgoing tenant pays thereafter. If there is any detail that has been overlooked we handle the extra cleaning and deduct the cost from the tenant's deposit by agreement.

27 Do you arrange the transfer of utility accounts?

We transfer gas / oil, electricity, water and council tax into the tenant's name and we pay your closing accounts, deducting the amounts from your rental income.

If there is a void period between tenancies, we transfer the accounts back into your name, then into the next tenant's name. Any small interim amount will be shown on your rental statement.

The procedure is different for the telephone landline account: British Telecom will not deal with agents, you need to let them know of your end-date.

However, we can actually pay the bill if you give BT instructions. Once you have terminated your account, you will probably lose the telephone number.

Short lets or tenancies to large companies often include utilities as part of the rent, so they remain in your name. In this situation, we add a generous margin in consultation with you. Telephones are excluded.

Property Management – During the Tenancy

28 How can I control the expenditure on my property?

The simple answer is: trust your agent.

But we realise it's not always as easy as that; so until we at Finders Keepers have earned your trust, here are some other solutions:

i.   Recognise and be prepared for the fact that tenants are less tolerant of problems than owners, and (justifiably) less willing to have a go at fixing something themselves. Mark Buckley, our MD for 25 years, always used the car analogy: tenants are like oil in your car – they show up any weak spots quickly. Showers may suddenly leak or have heat or flow issues, but often a complaint about a non-functioning oven is due to something small such as the timer needing resetting. This is where having an experienced agent really helps: at Finders Keepers we know to judge when to send out a contractor or go to inspect it ourselves first.

ii. Agree to a repairs limit. This allows your agent to deal with small problems quickly, without needing your approval. You can then think carefully about how you deal with bigger, more expensive problems, should they arise. Having said that, at Finders Keepers we will always try to get your consent to any expenditure because we know that repairs deplete your monthly rental income.

iii. Be realistic. The older the property, especially the interior and fittings, the greater the likelihood of repairs becoming necessary.

iv. Keep your rental property as well maintained as your own home (it may, of course, be your home if you are letting it whilst living elsewhere). This definitely reduces repairs to the absolute minimum.

v.   Finally, ensure that you arrange to meet your Property Manager at the property at least once a year to see for yourself what needs replacing, redecorating or updating. At Finders Keepers this means we can plan ahead with you so that any work is carried out as cost effectively as possible.

29 How often do you inspect the property?

We inspect properties at least twice yearly for Investor service clients, and three times for Home-Owners. In addition, we like to meet each landlord at their property once a year for their peace of mind, to minimise the 'old friend has changed' shock (see Question 44), and to discuss any maintenance needed.

If the property is being maintained in poor condition, we will communicate with the tenant and re-inspect. Almost always, this has the desired effect and house-keeping standards improve.

An essential part of our inspection is taking note of any unreported maintenance issues such as an overflow running, a gutter leaking or a missing roof tile. Many tenants fail to notice slow-burning issues (damp and black spot mould are two classics).

Obviously we can't predict emergency situations such as break-ins, floods, or fire (this is very rare). But if we do spot any problem at all, however small, we visit as often as necessary to be sure that it is put right; in the most urgent situations we will visit daily – but that is very seldom necessary.

What we can't do is keep the property under constant vigilance – unlike some well-intentioned neighbours. Brief your neighbours to contact us (not you) if they have any concerns. Invariably, neighbours exaggerate problems and add fuel to the fire. This can seriously jeopardise the tenants' goodwill.

30 How can I trust an agent's contractors? Can I use my own?

Good contractors are essential if you want to fix problems quickly and effectively, and keep your tenants happy.

Being able to trust contractors comes down to four criteria: technical skill, price, legal and response time.

The **technical** skills are non-negotiable – both for simple handyman work (broken door handles) and complex problems (damp, broken boilers). You also need a Property Manager with the depth of experience to have technical conversations with contractors.

At Finders Keepers we assess the technical skills of new contractors by taking references and then giving them a couple of jobs. We inspect the work closely and decide if they are good enough. Contractors are only human and standards can go up and down. If standards fall, then we will address the problem immediately.

We have contractors who work almost solely for us and have done for 10+ years. They know the high standards we expect and, in return, they can count on us to pay their invoices promptly.

We also use the large amount of work we commission to negotiate the best **prices**. These are benchmarked each year as rates do go up and down according to the health of the economy. As with many services, you get what you pay for.

If you think you are paying too much, ask your Property Manager to explain the costs, but realise you have a duty of care to provide a safe, working property

for your tenant. We had one landlord who said: *"Why do they need hot water? I shower in cold water."* If you empathise with that view, you will not be a successful landlord.

The **legal** question is that each contractor must have valid public liability insurance. If they do not, you should not use them. We stop paying invoices if their insurance runs out – that soon solves the problem!

Response time is a huge factor. Some landlords do not care about this as they are not the ones living with the problem – their tenants are. But they should care enough to make sure that their agents use only contractors who can respond swiftly.

Finally, of course you can use your **own contractors**. Tell your agent when you first sign up. Just make sure that your contractors have their public liability insurance and bear in mind that you, rather than your agent, will need to pay their invoices.

31 How quickly do I have to repair faults?

All faults should be repaired quickly.
If a part is needed and is on order, it is important that we explain about this to the tenant and schedule in fitting it on the earliest possible date.

The motto in these cases is "do as you would be done by" and you should act especially urgently to deal with breakdowns in essential services: heating, hot water, and electricity.

The most frequent and upsetting situation for a tenant is when a continuous feed boiler breaks down, resulting in no heating or hot water. In such cases we often have to re-house the tenants temporarily, although all offices have a supply of electric convection heaters that we can lend tenants. We make separate

arrangements for using local showers when feasible.

When the diagnosis is that a new boiler is needed – costing several thousand pounds – we have to obtain the owner's consent for the expenditure. If this should happen to you, do not delay your approval.

You have a statutory obligation to maintain essential services at all times. Failure to do this could result in the tenant successfully claiming damages. This is why we go to great lengths to deal with breakdowns as soon as they happen.

Legislation is changing regarding the section 21 notice where there is outstanding maintenance work. If you refuse to repair faults you run the risk of not being able to serve a section 21 notice.

32 What happens if there is an emergency out-of-hours?

At Finders Keepers, we make sure that a member of our staff is 'on call' for each of our offices at all times. Tenants have the out-of-hours emergency number on a card which they receive upon moving in.

Emergency Service Card
01865 311011 **FindersKeepers**

- The out of office hours emergency service is for FK tenants in a managed property
- Follow the instructions and you will be given a number of options which connect to a voicemail service
- Leave your name, telephone number, address and details of the emergency problem
- You will be contacted shortly

What is an 'emergency'?
The Finders Keepers 24/7 line is for genuine emergencies only such as a bad leak, flood, fire or an unforeseen crisis such as a break-in.

The following are common calls but are not always emergencies:

"I have lost my keys" We can try to get a locksmith out, but this cannot be guaranteed late at night and is a tenant cost, not a landlord cost.

"My electricity has gone" Nine times out of ten this is the trip switch and we talk people through correcting it.

"The alarm is sounding" We try to get the alarm company out immediately to switch it off. They also work out if the cause is tenant error or product error.

"I cannot work my cooker / fridge, etc." We find that referring people to the manual (hard copy or online) normally works.

What we do
Whenever possible, we send out a contractor after discussing the situation with the tenant. We may visit in person if it is safe to do so.

Emergencies are fortunately rare, but having an experienced member of staff on call minimises risk and damage and gives everyone some peace of mind.

We are the only company that we know of that does not outsource this very important service to a call-centre. Many letting agents do not offer an emergency service at all. One very famous agent just gives tenants a list of contractor details and asks them to handle it themselves. This is all very well, but who handles the complaints when the landlord refuses to pay the bills for non-emergencies?

If you are managing the property
Then you need to handle emergencies 24/7, or not – it is your decision and they are your tenants to keep happy. Bear in mind that if you fail to respond to emergency calls, then your property might incur further damage, e.g. if there is a leak.

33 Can I come and do some work on my property during the tenancy?

We strongly recommend doing any work *before* the tenancy starts or *between* tenancies.

If you have renewed the tenancy and the tenant has been in occupation for two or more years, it is understandable that you might want to carry out some repairs or maintenance. Occasionally, a tenant will agree to the work being done during his or her absence on holiday, but this can't be guaranteed. If you want to carry out work while the tenant is there, proceed with caution because the tenant is legally entitled to the 'quiet enjoyment of the property'.

- However charming and tactful you are, the tenant is likely to feel your presence as an invasion of privacy. (Subconsciously there is always some territorial conflict between landlord and tenant.) Sending in a qualified contractor, a neutral third party, is a much better solution.

- If you really must do the work yourself, then enlist the help of another person to partially diffuse any possibility of territorial irritation.

- Although you may feel certain you will avoid any comments which may upset the tenant, it can be very difficult if you think *your* property / home is not being as well cared for as if you lived there. This especially applies to gardens. If your garden maintenance matters greatly, then employing a gardener and including the cost in the rent is essential to avoid future problems.

- Don't ever visit without giving the required 24 hours' notice specified in the tenancy agreement.

- Beware of well-meaning neighbours' critical comments which can greatly inflame a situation.

Best of all, leave it to your agent to instruct contractors on your behalf. At Finders Keepers we are experienced at arranging ongoing work at a convenient time for the tenant or tactfully putting across your opinion. Bricks & Mortar, our building division, has excellent, approved sub-contractors.

But if you really can't afford a professional contractor and want to carry out major work yourself, then it is probably better to end the tenancy early, by mutual agreement.

34 If I provide a TV or white goods am I responsible for repairing them when they 'break down'?

Unless misuse can be proved, as the landlord you are responsible for repairs to all white goods and electrical items provided by you. This rule applies to every component of a letting, i.e. to everything that appears on the inventory.

Nowadays **white goods** are usually included in kitchens when they are fitted; only in older style kitchens is there a slot-in space, and so appliances are expected. Tenants resent having to buy them. Not providing them makes letting all the harder.

Televisions are *not* expected except in serviced or short lets. They reduce in price each year and are an item that many tenants enjoy buying.

If you are buying a TV for a rental, John Lewis sets have a five-year warranty which we have used on several occasions and saved clients money on ensuing repairs.

35 What causes condensation and who is responsible for removing the mould?

What is condensation?

Condensation occurs when water vapour in the air condenses into a liquid, for example, during the winter on to glass windows. It is a real issue between October and April as the external air temperature falls and water from the air forms as condensation on cold surfaces such as windows and external walls. Everyone has heard the horror stories of bathrooms and kitchens with marked ceilings and window sills as condensation turns into black mould growth, but explaining to tenants that the cause is most probably due to their lifestyle – rather than underlying problems with the property – is not always an easy conversation.

The biggest hurdle is in explaining something invisible to someone. Water in the air from cooking, washing and showering is clearly visible as steam, but there is also much more water in the air that you cannot see, especially in areas where the water table is fairly close to the ground (as it is in Oxford) rather than buried many metres below it. This 'invisible' water content is just waiting to condense on a cold window or north-facing wall.

Why does condensation arise?

1. Too much moisture in the property

- Breathing – 2 adults sleeping in an unventilated room for 8 hours release an average of 1.5 pints of moisture into the atmosphere.

- Cooking – Cooking on the hob or boiling a kettle can produce up to 6 pints of moisture. Steam condenses on colder surfaces, exterior walls, tiles and windows.

- Bathrooms and Laundry – This can produce up to 11 pints of moisture which may spread around the house and not just remain in the bathroom or utility room.

2. Not enough ventilation

- Ventilation helps to remove moist air by replacing it with drier air from outside.

- This normally fails when there is no extractor fan fitted in the bathroom or when the fan has a separate switch which the tenant turns off.

3. Putting on the heating with no ventilation

- Warm air holds more moisture than cooler air. Air is like a sponge: the warmer it is, the more moisture it will hold. Heating one room to a high level and leaving others cold makes condensation worse in the unheated rooms.

How do I stop mould and avoid being charged to remove it?

Generally, the tenant will be charged to get rid of mould as it arises from condensation which in turn is caused by tenant behaviour. Following all the instructions mentioned here should prevent mould occurring. Mould can be wiped off with a proprietary fungicidal wash that is available from supermarkets. Make sure it carries a Health and Safety Executive (HSE) approval number and that you follow instructions for its safe use.

How to stop condensation

- Open windows and trickle vents! Even keeping a small window open will make a big difference.

- Use and maintain extractor fans in kitchens and bathrooms and keep doors closed.

- Dry washing outside where possible. Open a window if drying washing indoors or use a tumble dryer.

- Ventilate cupboards and wardrobes – do not overfill. Let the air circulate freely.

- Wipe water from windows and sills where condensation has gathered.

- Draw back curtains in all rooms every day to avoid staining the linings.

36 What happens if my tenant sub-lets?
What if they get a pet without permission?

Both would be breaches of covenants by the tenant. As with any breach, you or your agent should write to the tenant, remind them that they have broken the terms of their tenancy agreement, and ask them to put it right. Remember to follow up to check that they have done so.

Sub-letting is becoming more common, as people seek an additional source of income. However, many tenancy agreements, and certainly the Finders Keepers agreement, prohibit sub-letting. This is why regular inspections of the property are a must, to ensure the tenant is complying with the terms of the tenancy agreement.

Having said that, it's unlikely that sub-letting would be grounds for eviction: that would be up to the discretion of the Judge, were

you to take it to court. Often a conversation with the tenant and a reminder in writing is enough to put a stop to it. There potentially may be more legislation on this in future.

Pets. We have often come across evidence of pets being kept in rental properties against the terms of the tenancy agreement – cat food hidden in the airing cupboard, for example, or dogs locked in parked cars at the specific time that we have been asked to visit to carry out an inspection. Again, though, in order to evict a tenant for keeping a pet you would have to take them to court and prove that they have broken the terms of their agreement. Even then, the Judge may not agree with you. Talking to the tenant is usually the best way to resolve this problem.

In fact, it might be worth deciding to accept pets in your property, although usually pets are prohibited in apartments under the terms of the head lease. As the private rental sector is growing, we are seeing more families with pets applying as tenants. It's important to take each application on its own merit of course: one cocker spaniel with its owner at home all day is a very different proposition to four German Shepherds with an owner who works full time! When pets are accepted, we always take a higher deposit and separately negotiate additional clauses relating to cleaning and damage for the tenancy agreement.

37 How quickly can you evict a tenant?

These situations are rare.There has been a lot of publicity in the national and trade media about evictions. There is quite a lot of protection for the tenants regarding evictions and landlords need to tread carefully.

If the tenant – landlord relationship just doesn't work out

You won't be able to evict the tenant during the tenancy unless they have breached a covenant – that is, unless they have done something that they promised not to as part of your tenancy agreement. If they have not breached a covenant, you will have to wait until the end of the assured shorthold tenancy to get your property back, unless you can both agree an early termination.

Evicting the tenant yourself by changing the locks or removing the tenant's belongings (or instructing someone else to do so) is a criminal offence under the Protection from Eviction Act 1977.

If the tenant does not pay the rent

If the tenant owes two months' rent or more, you can take them to court. You will be guaranteed possession of your property providing they still have rent arrears of at least two months at the time of going to court. You should get a court hearing within one or two months of your application, and the Judge will then grant

you possession of your property within 14 to 42 days.

If the tenant has rent arrears of less than two months, or if they are consistently late with their payments, you can still take them to court. However, in such cases it is up to the Judge whether or not to grant you possession of your property. 'Eviction' is not guaranteed.

If the tenant damages the property

You can take the tenant to court for a breach of covenant, but you would need to prove that you told the tenant in writing how they broke the tenancy agreement and asked them to put the breach right before taking any legal action against them.

Even if you have this evidence, eviction is not guaranteed. A Judge may just place an order on the tenant to put matters right rather than give you possession.

It's hard to say how likely it is that a Judge would grant you possession of your property if a tenant damaged it. The Judge is likely to take into account what type of damage has been caused, how it has been caused, the length of the tenancy and the type and number of tenants. So you should think carefully and take advice before deciding to start court proceedings.

38 What would happen if a tenant didn't move out at the end of a tenancy?

This has become a worryingly pertinent question since the recession. Local authorities are struggling to provide social housing to those in need. Some are advising people on the social housing waiting list to stay in their rental property *beyond* the agreed end-date until they are evicted. This is not ethical (in our view) and it causes problems for the landlord and also the new incoming tenant, who cannot move in; it breaks the fundamental agreement between landlord and tenant.

Many landlords cannot believe that tenants can stay in a property without instant repercussions. But you cannot manhandle the tenants out of the property or intimidate them and so you must abide by the law.

The legal process
A section 21 notice (legally required under the Housing Act 1988) has to be served on the tenant no less than two months before the end of the tenancy if you want them to leave.

If a tenant fails to hand the property back on the last day of the tenancy, you will need to go to court and request an order for possession, which will always be granted under shorthold legislation. You cannot evict the tenant or change the locks yourself.

As mentioned in the previous question, providing the legal notice has been served on the tenant, a Judge will give you possession of the property between 14 and 42 days after the date of the hearing.

The terms of the tenancy continue for this 'additional' period so the tenant remains responsible for the rent payments until they leave.

39 Do students trash properties?

If you let them, yes! Students are young, excitable 19- to 23-year-olds. They are living away from home, feeling very grown-up, and paying just like any other tenant for their accommodation. And, of course, they are paying market rates. Nothing is discounted.

They will have parties, love affairs, break-ups and arguments. Some won't want to get up or go to lectures. They will endure hangovers as they come to terms with what their bodies can tolerate in a city that is more-or-less designed for drinking and late-night revelling. But students are often no worse than young families, when you have to cope with children's grubby hands all over the walls and toys bashed into skirting boards.

The key with all letting, but especially with student letting, is to prepare the property well in the first place.

- Buy strong, durable furniture – no flat-packed furniture or sofas with silly legs – you don't want to imagine what student sofas endure!

- Manage students carefully. Keep a light touch, but make sure you're always there somewhere in their subconscious.

- Conduct detailed, thorough inventories and inspections. It's no good leaving everything to the Check Out, especially as deposit schemes are usually lenient towards students.

- Avoid end-of-tenancy disputes at all costs and involve parents or guarantors as soon as possible if cleanliness or damage issues need addressing.

- Better still: employ a dedicated student Property Manager.

40 When can I put the rent up?

Rent levels are close to the hearts of both landlords and tenants, who usually have different views on the subject.

There are two main factors: legal requirements and market forces. Successful landlords obey the former and work with the latter.

Can I put the rent up during a tenancy?
In a word: no. An Assured Shorthold Tenancy (AST) guarantees the tenant the right to occupy your property in exchange for paying the rent (this is a simplification, but the premise still stands). The amount of rent is fixed and cannot be changed during a tenancy unless *both* parties agree.

Can I put the rent up if my tenant surrenders his tenancy?
We would advise against it. A 'surrender' is when your tenant wants to leave their tenancy before the end of it. They are still legally liable for the rent until the property is re-let. We advise re-marketing the property at the same rent: if you ask for more rent than the tenant is paying, it may prevent re-letting, and this would not be seen as fair if the surrendering tenant brought the case up for review. If there is little demand due to the time of year, you may need to lower the asking rent and the surrendering tenant will be liable for the difference between their rent and the incoming tenant's rent.

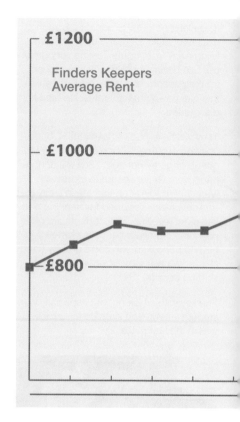

£1200

Finders Keepers
Average Rent

£1000

£800

What rent increase am I getting this year?
You cannot assume that you will always get a rent increase. ASTs do not have clauses stating that rent reviews only go up – they are unlike 'upward only' commercial rent clauses.

If you run fixed-term tenancy agreements (as we do), then you renegotiate the rent upon renewing the tenancy. You put a

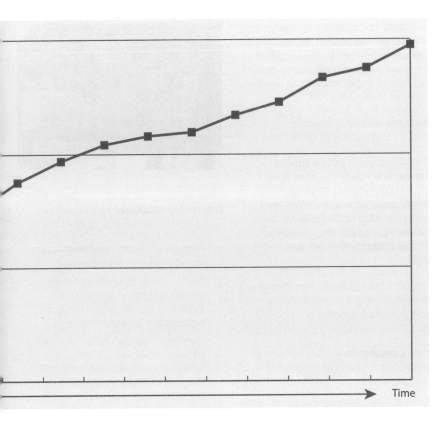

Time

rent to the tenant and they can accept or decline it; it is a negotiation in which market forces are the guide.

Can I build rent increases into the original tenancy agreement?
Yes, we do this and it works well. Normally we put an 'RPI increase' clause in every 12 months.

Can I put the rent up if the tenancy has gone Periodic?
Yes. You need to issue the correct legal notice to warn the tenant and you must give them at least one rent payment period's notice. The tenant can respond with their own legal notice if they do not agree. From there it is a negotiation which, if not settled, can go to the First-Tier Tribunal, which is rare.

41 How would a fire or accident affect my liability or reputation?

Our corporate and institutional clients ask about these issues a lot. Most letting markets are quite small ecosystems and landlords are aware that they carry certain responsibilities. Landlords want to know that risks are being mitigated.

Our response splits into insurance, compliance and day-to-day behaviour.

Every landlord needs **public liability insurance**. This is why you need specific landlord insurance that combines buildings, public liability and often legal insurance. So if the unthinkable happens – for example, a tenant trips on a carpet and injures himself – then you are covered.

Ask us about our landlord policy through Jelf Insurance – it is a thorough, proven policy which offers everything a landlord needs.

Accurate **compliance** is a big part of risk mitigation. Our Property Managers know their obligations:

1. Gas – an annual inspection is compulsory by law.
2. Electrical safety – this is (amazingly) not compulsory, but it should be. A fixed wiring test lasts for five years and is worth every penny.
3. Fire – furniture needs to pass regulations.
4. Smoke and CO detectors – not compulsory, but good landlords fit them.
5. HMOs – these have their own Health and Safety requirements.

Day-to-day behaviour by landlord and agent influences reputation, for example:

1. Attitude to repairs – delaying repairs causes negative word-of-mouth.
2. Noise – noisy tenants can create serious reputational damage for landlords. Our Property Managers tackle noise issues immediately.
3. Disrepair – slovenly properties are bad for your reputation, e.g. when bins are allowed to get out of control. Our Property Managers carry out thorough inspections and respond to neighbour complaints.

Allowing people to live in your properties in exchange for rent is not without risks, but we are here to mitigate and manage the risks for you. Strong policies, robust systems and large dollops of common sense help us tackle the issues as they arise.

42 What should I do if I want to sell my rental property?

If you want to sell your rental property, then you should start by asking yourself two questions:

1. Do I want to sell it with a tenant *in situ*? There is no right or wrong answer. For some properties an existing tenant is an asset and helps to sell the property to a landlord who wants to 'buy income'. For other properties it can deter buyers.

2. Is the timing right re capital gains tax? We recommend mentioning the sale to your accountant just to check that you are optimising your tax planning.

Talk to us about 1. and we can give you the names of several reliable accountants for 2.

In fact, your first port of call should always be your letting agent. They will be able to speak to your tenants and see if they might be interested in buying the property. Even if they are not interested, it will still help to have them on board for viewings. Lack of sensitivity from Estate Agents often causes problems with viewing access, which we are used to resolving.

Your agent will be able to:

- Arrange for valuations of the property from a suitable number of local agents, making sure that they are the right agents for the property. Choosing the right agent is probably the most important part of selling: you wouldn't go to an Aston Martin dealer to buy a Vauxhall, for example.

- Liaise with the tenants to arrange viewings. Remember that selling a let property is nowhere near as straightforward as selling your own home, when you will probably do anything to help with the sale. Your tenants are paying for the right to live in the property and they can make the viewing progress quite painful if they are not dealt with respectfully.

- Negotiate the terms of the sale with the agent on your behalf, and recommend local solicitors. Remember that professional letting agents are experienced negotiators and will be able to secure the best possible result for you.

- Help you to find a new property if you want to re-invest the money from the sale.

PROPERTY MANAGEMENT –
DURING THE TENANCY

After the
Tenancy

43 How do you assess damage?

At the end of a tenancy, you may deduct money from the returnable deposit to cover damaged or missing items. But remember that you must stick to the strict rules laid down by the Government-backed deposit protection schemes. In law the deposit remains the property of the tenant.

You cannot make deductions for the full replacement value of an item: you have to take normal wear and tear into account, as well as the item's quality and condition at the start of the tenancy.

- If an item is damaged, but not so badly that it needs to be replaced, then you can make a deduction to compensate for the damage and the reduction in the item's lifespan.
- If an item is missing, the cost of replacing it should be based on its second-hand value at the end of the tenancy.
- Even if the damage appears to be deliberate, it will not cost more to repair than accidental damage. So you can't hold back more than a fair contribution towards making good or replacing the item.

This is why it is vital to have a thorough inventory – including photos – of all items in the property. Invoices showing the original cost of the items or manufacturer's guarantees can also be useful in establishing an item's age and quality.

Why can't I have new for old?

If you want 'new for old', you are expecting a tenant to pay the full cost of a new replacement (with its increased lifespan, lower maintenance costs, warranties etc.) for something that was not new when the tenancy started. This is referred to as 'betterment', meaning that you have gained financially more than you would have expected to at the end of the tenancy.

How do I determine how long decoration and carpets should last?

Although only a general guide, the information in the table may be a useful starting point when making allowance for fair wear and tear. This gauge is approximate and assumes an averagely sized property with average use.

Table 1: **Average lifespan of decoration**

Hall, landing, stairs:	approx 2 – 3 years
Living rooms:	approx 4 years
Dining rooms:	approx 6 years
Kitchen & bathrooms:	approx 2 – 3 years
Bedrooms:	approx 5 years

Table 2: **Average lifespan of carpets**

Budget:	approx 3 – 5 years
Medium quality:	approx 5 – 10 years
Top quality:	up to 20 years

44 After all this work, can I expect to receive my property back in the same condition?

Yes and no!

Yes, as your agent we will ensure that everything is restored to the condition described in the inventory, which includes photographs.

No, because, the longer the time the property is let, the greater the wear and tear which is allowed under the British Tenancy Law.

Successful landlords understand that wear and tear is a cost of doing business just as fuel is a cost for FedEx and DHL.

Be prepared
Wear and tear is like meeting an old friend and being surprised to discover that he or she has aged.

This is a difficult concept for some landlords to accept. They don't notice the gentle deterioration of their *own* home as they live in it full time, but they pounce on changes to a rental property they have not seen for several years. This is not reasonable.

Some of the biggest and most surprising changes happen in gardens. One family barely recognised their garden when they returned to their house after 15 years. It was a new house when they left with just a lawn. Plants and shrubs they had paid for had matured and grown over the years.

Moving forward
If you haven't redecorated for several years, the condition will have deteriorated, even with the most house-proud of tenants. If you are letting to a family with children, the property will have suffered even more wear and tear. The Tenancy Deposit Scheme advises that high-traffic areas (kitchen, hallways, bathrooms) need redecorating every three years.

Sometimes we are disappointed with aspects of the final presentation of family homes. But it is part of our service to ensure that everything is put right (less wear and tear). The inventory is the document used by all parties to evaluate any deductions from the tenants' deposit.

Reassuringly, Finders Keepers founder Mary Channer cannot remember a single case in 45 years of a tenant completely wrecking a rental property.

Damage, however, does happen. Normally it is accidental and not malicious, but there isn't really much point in arguing about the cause: our job is to make sure that the damage is put right.

Damage during a tenancy
When we are managing a property, we carry out two or three inspections each year, depending on the service. This is not an audit of the inventory, but if we see damage to the property or its contents, we will tackle it and resolve the matter. If that forces an unpleasant issue into the open, that is good – it is better to address problems early than leave them to the Check Out.

We try to establish good relationships with our tenants so that they tell us if they damage something.

Damage at the end of a tenancy
Often damage does not come to light until the end of a tenancy. This is for two main reasons:

- The tenant has not reported it. One person's major damage can be another person's minor irritation.
- It is only at the end of a tenancy that a thorough audit of the Inventory is carried out.

The Inventory is critical: we compare the state of the property and items at the Check Out to what is described in the Inventory and reconcile the differences.

Damage is usually minor. We see things such as broken glasses, faulty door handles, chips to plaster and broken shelves. More problematical are stains to carpets, marks on walls, dead or dying plants in the garden or bare patches on the lawn, and damage to kitchen worktops. None of these constitute 'wrecking' the place.

What we do come across, though – once or twice a year – is a landlord who is dissatisfied with what we professionally consider to be fair wear and tear. In such cases, extensive correspondence and numerous meetings lead to a mutually satisfying conclusion. All part of the job!

Tax and Financial

46 Am I correctly insured on my let property?

When you let out your property, it is essential that you insure it with a specific Landlord's Policy. While traditional household insurance covers a property against risks such as fire, flood and theft, it does not allow for the additional risks which come with having tenants. Specialist insurance policies will provide buildings and contents cover for the owners of tenant-occupied properties, as well as cover for risks such as Landlord's Liability and loss of rent. You can also include legal expenses and a rent guarantee in these policies.

It is worth noting that your tenants are responsible for protecting their own belongings against loss or damage.

However small your property, and however few properties you own, you must have proper landlord insurance. If you are letting out a house or flat that was once your home, it is vital that you inform your existing insurer and make sure that you have the correct policy. Your previous household insurance is likely to be invalid.

A good landlord's insurance policy typically offers the following cover:

- All Risks for building and contents
- Accidental Damage and Malicious Damage
- Landlord's Liability
- Loss of Rent following an insured event (for example, if a flood makes a house temporarily uninhabitable)
- Legal Expenses
- Optional Rent Guarantee

Some insurers are happy to make arrangements for the agents to pay premiums on your behalf and deal quickly with small claims without having to ask for multiple quotes.

We have helped develop a very good policy with Jelf Insurance. Ask us for details.

47 Can you guarantee the rent?
Will Finders Keepers pay the rent if the tenant doesn't?

Finders Keepers works with a partner (Jelf Insurance) to offer rent guarantee insurance.

So, yes, we can 'guarantee the rent', but, to be clear, an insurance company does the guaranteeing and they will pay the rent if the tenant doesn't.

Read the Terms and Conditions
Any rent guarantee product will have Terms and Conditions and these can vary dramatically. You must *fully understand* the small print on any product you buy. Common T&Cs include:

- The first month's rent is not included – as the deposit should cover it.
- There will be a limit to the amount of rent that can be guaranteed, e.g. £2,500 pcm.
- There will be a limit to the length of time that rent will be covered, e.g. no more than six months. So you will get months two, three, four, five and six paid. The theory behind this is that if you need to evict someone for not paying the rent, by month six you should have a new tenant in your property.

Why do I need rent guarantee insurance if Finders Keepers is so good at collecting the rent?
A fair question – at Finders Keepers we are proud of our 99+% rent collection track record. We are tactful, persistent and accurate when chasing the rent.

However, some landlords want that extra peace of mind. Life is unpredictable and, no matter how thorough our referencing is, major life events such as redundancy, debt, illness and divorce can affect someone's ability to pay the rent. We have many landlords who feel that the rent guarantee product is a small price to pay for knowing that the vast majority of their income is protected.

48 What sort of expenses are tax-deductible?

You can deduct expenses against tax as long they are genuinely for the letting of the property. They have to be revenue expenses (i.e. running costs) and cannot be capital expenses (i.e. set-up costs and improvements).

What are revenue expenses?
Expenses which can be claimed against tax include letting agents' fees and the direct costs of letting the property, such as the administration and advertising costs. For mortgage payments, the interest charges can be allowed, but the capital repayment element is not tax-deductible. Additional revenue expenses include buildings and contents insurance, service charges and ground rent, gardening expenses, legal/agreement fees and any other services not paid for by the tenant, such as council tax, utilities, water rates, cleaning and repairs and maintenance. As a landlord you may be able to deduct the cost of your travel if it is genuine business travel.

What is classed as a repair?
The simple rule is that a repair is something that keeps the property in the same condition it was in when it was first let. Anything that makes it better than when it was first let is an improvement, and you can't claim improvements against income tax.

Common repair expenses are exterior and interior painting and decorating, mending broken windows, doors, furniture and machines, such as washing machines, and stone cleaning. Replacement kitchens and bathrooms can be claimed too as long as there is no substantial upgrade. HMRC also allow for the cost

of replacing single-glazed windows with double glazing, even though that could be seen as an improvement. Remember that improvements to the property are treated as capital expenses and potentially included in any capital gains tax calculation if the property is eventually sold. Ask your accountant for more detail.

Are there any other deductible expenses which I should know about?
Yes, for furnished lettings you can claim a 'wear and tear' allowance. This is calculated by taking 10% of the rent, less charges or services. It covers items such as furniture, soft furnishings, white goods, crockery and cutlery — so you can't claim any more for these items.

However, if the property is let unfurnished, then you cannot claim the 'wear and tear' allowance. Nor are you able to deduct the cost of replacements or of adding any new items into the property for the first time.

The important thing about expenses is to keep accurate and up-to-date records.

49 I live overseas, but my property is in Oxfordshire; how does this affect the tax I pay?

If you are a landlord receiving UK rental income and you live outside the UK for more than six months of the year, you are classed as 'non-resident' for tax purposes. This also applies to the armed forces, companies and trustees based outside the UK.

You are still liable for UK tax, but there can be some flexibility in how the tax is paid.

You must have an HMRC 'Approval number' before we (your letting agent) can remit your rent to you without tax being deducted.

To get an Approval Number
Individual landlords apply for this Approval number at **www.hmrc.gov.uk/cnr/nrl1.pdf**

If you own your property jointly with another non-resident, such as your spouse, they will need to apply for approval independently.

Companies apply via
www.hmrc.gov.uk/cnr/nrl2.pdf
Trustees via
www.hmrc.gov.uk/cnr/nrl3.pdf

When approval has been given, HMRC will send a notice both to you and to your letting agent, authorising your agent to pay rent to you without deducting tax. This rent remains liable to UK tax, and you must include it in any tax return that HMRC sends you. Take advice from an accountant if you are in doubt.

If you do not have an Approval number
Your letting agent must by law deduct tax from your net rental income (that is, your total rental income minus allowable expenses) and pay it to HMRC on your behalf.

Your letting agent will pay this tax on a quarterly basis. At the end of the tax year, they will send you a tax certificate that shows all the tax paid on your behalf. You can then set this against the tax you owe when you complete your self-assessment tax return.

If you live abroad and manage the property yourself you will need to check with HMRC or your accountant on how your tenant should pay the rent.